PRAISE FOR
SATAN TALKS TO HIS THERAPIST

"In one of the wickedly funny poems from *Satan Talks to His Therapist*, Dorothy Parker's ghost drops in to comment on a political situation. Don't believe it for a second, because if Parker's ghost were to visit a Balmain poem, she would likely set fire to it out of spiteful envy. Melissa Balmain is the once and future Queen of American light verse, and only a ghost could keep from laughing all the way through this marvelous collection."

> **—Julie Kane, former Louisiana Poet Laureate
> and author of *Mothers of Ireland***

"Melissa Balmain's poems use precision without derision. She's a master at the craft of verse—and her incisive wit and rueful intelligence make this book a profound read. This book takes on varied sources of contemporary angst: COVID-19, aging as a woman in a consumer culture, Zoom recitals, and medical mysteries. If the LOLSOB emoji could write verse that both sings and stings, the result would be *Satan Talks to His Therapist*. Highly recommended for poets and those who think poetry has nothing to do with modern life—Melissa Balmain's poems will make converts of us all."

> **—Allison Joseph, author of *Confessions of a
> Barefaced Woman***

"It turns out that the literary establishment can't quite kill off humorous poetry. Melissa Balmain's *Satan Talks to His Therapist* is a marvel in the tradition of Martial, Jonathan Swift, and Dorothy Parker and the more recent generation of poets that includes Wendy Cope, X. J. Kennedy and R. S. Gwynn. It is poetry you will enjoy—and enjoy giving to a friend who needs to see some humor in a world desperate for the medicine of laughter."

—A.M. Juster, author of *Wonder and Wrath*

"Like Jonathan Swift, Melissa Balmain is a deft metrist and a delightfully inventive rhymer, whose wit is enriched by a great heart. In *Satan Talks to His Therapist*, she captures the disorientations of the Age of Trump and COVID-19, satirizing the meanness and sympathizing with the suffering. Though the outstanding poems here are too numerous to list, special treasures include 'On Looking at an MRI Cross-Section,' the title poem, 'Niagara Overlook,' and 'Reprieve.'"

—Timothy Steele, author of *Toward the Winter Solstice*

"I can't convey the essence of *Satan Talks to His Therapist*; it's Balmain's language itself that captures contemporary idiom like no other poet I know. Parody is one of her specialties: Don't gather rosebuds, she advises—just call 1-800-FLOWERS. For Balmain, words and wit are one."

—Deborah Warren, author of *Connoisseurs of Worms*

"Melissa was probably funny straight out of the womb, with a huge internal rhyming dictionary, a fearless vocabulary, a scary gift for hilarious imagery, and instantaneous recognition of, and attraction to, the absurd. But her most valuable gift is easy to miss: it's the capacity to tell the truth, even about the irritating—the even unforgivable!—without the verbal mean streak that normally accompanies humor. Even her Satan defends himself ("Life isn't fair!" he exclaims) with a touch of dignity; the gun lover loves his weapon so passionately that we almost see his point as he aims it at us; and as for family and friends, their most annoying foibles—excessive knickknacks everywhere, the advantages of some at the bland expense of others, slurping soup noises, birdsong at inconvenient times—are all fully revealed (except when the beloved slurper is sick) and are never denied at least a measure of slack. This poet's best gift is a limitless supply of patience—or maybe it's love—that extends even to life's many unavoidables: nature, the human race, and her own failings, which the poet confesses with a smile not only visible but audible in the very music of her work."

— **Rhina P. Espaillat, author of** *And After All*

OTHER PRAISE FOR MELISSA BALMAIN

"Melissa Balmain is the finest light poet in America."

— **Michael Gerber, Editor and Publisher of**
The American Bystander

On *Walking in on People* **(winner of**
the Able Muse Book Award):

"Melissa Balmain's poems add to the rhythmic bounce of light verse a darker, more cutting humor. The result is an infectious, often hilarious blend of the sweet and the lethal, the charming and the acidic."

— **Billy Collins, former U.S. Poet Laureate**

"*Walking in on People* grabbed me with its very title, and it never let go. Poetry these days is rarely so entertaining, so beautifully crafted, so sharp of eye, yet so wise and warm of heart. Melissa Balmain keenly perceives faults in people and in our popular culture, with piercing wit but never bitterness."

— **X. J. Kennedy, winner of the Robert Frost Medal**

"Most of Balmain's poems are not light in the sense of frivolous or superficial. They often raise serious topics, but they do so with a wonderful sense of humor. . . . If you are wanting to convert someone who thinks reading poetry is only a slight improvement over visiting the dentist, get him or her this book."

— ***Expansive Poetry Online***

"So many of the poems in Melissa Balmain's triumphant debut lodge themselves in that Frostian zone where they are hard to get rid of. They recur in the mind in moments of hilarity and pathos, of exaltation and mortification, and they never let us go."

—**David Yezzi, author of *More Things in Heaven***

On *The Witch Demands a Retraction: Fairy Tale Reboots for Adults*:

"A typically devilishly delightful new book by . . . Melissa Balmain."

—**Pat Myers in *The Washington Post***

"Does anyone say, 'OH NO SHE DI-INT!' anymore? Because that will be your response to basically every poem in this treat of a book. Balmain turns every fairy tale on its head and shows us its panties, none the worse for wear. Just don't be drinking anything while you read, because these verses are a recipe for spit takes. Balmain has a warped mind and astonishing wit matched thoroughly by her warm heart."

—**Faith Salie, comedian, author, journalist seen & heard on CBS, NPR & PBS**

"Witty, cringey, and hilarious."

—**Tom Bodett, author and NPR personality**

SATAN TALKS TO
HIS THERAPIST

SATAN TALKS TO HIS THERAPIST

Melissa Balmain

PAUL DRY BOOKS

Philadelphia 2023

First Paul Dry Books Edition, 2023

Paul Dry Books, Inc.
Philadelphia, Pennsylvania
www.pauldrybooks.com

Printed in the United States of America

Library of Congress Control Number: 2023938619

ISBN: 978-1-58988-181-5

For Judy, Lucille, Rhina, and Mae—
the ones I want to be when I grow up

Contents

Climbing Out

Acknowledgments

Many thanks to the publications and websites that gave many poems in this book their first home:

The American Bystander: "Five Ages of Woman," "We Make the Mask," "Contingency Plan," "Coronostalgia," "Sidewalk Face-Off," "Satan Talks to His Therapist," "Preposterous," "Native Fauna," "The Test," "When the Chips Are Down . . . ," "Coffee Drinking Linked to Lower Mortality Risk, New Study Finds," "Bubble Rap," "The Sheltering Suburbanite to Her Neighbor," "Vaxxed Life," "Why This Is the Poem of Mine That People Will Share When I Die"

The Asses of Parnassus: "Tit for Tat: One-Syll Tips for Pols," "Philip Larkin Tries for a Vaccine Appointment"

Calamaro: "Reprieve"

Ecotone: "In the Beeswax Room"

The Hopkins Review: "Thumbelina Moves On"

Lighten Up Online: "Fruit and Consequences," "The Upside of Grief," "William Shakespeare (@ShakespeareWi) is now following you on Twitter!" "Invasive Species," "To the Blue Jay that Woke Me Every Morning—Until the Day I Leaned Out My Window and Roared, and It Flew Away in a Panic," "Morning Report," "To

My Son, Upon Removal of One of My Ovaries," "Being the parent . . . ," "Memo to Self, in Middle Age," "Fallen," "Best in Show," "Understatement," "Public Relations," "Zoom Recital: Gallery View," "Moonshine," "A Literal-Minded Virgin Reads Robert Herrick," "Undergrowth," "Jingle for a Law Firm," "To My Husband, Re My Tennis Elbow," "Birdwatching"

Literary Matters: "To Mom, in the Beyond"

McSweeney's Internet Tendency: "What Dylan Thomas Would Say if He Were Around for National Donut Day"

Mezzo Cammin: "To-Do," "My Mother's Ghost Whispers in My Ear at Starbucks," "Getting Spammed by Wendy Cope's Hacked Email Account"

Nasty Women Poets: An Unapologetic Anthology of Subversive Verse (Lost Horse Press): "Dorothy Parker's Ghost Weighs in on the 'New Political Climate'"

The New Criterion: "Treasure Map"

The New Verse News: "Thanksgiving Climate Change Song," "Fatal Mistakes," "Wednesday in Mount Hope Cemetery," "Breaking," "My Thoughts and Prayers Go Out to You," "Uncombable," "Blue-Plate Special"

The website of *Poetry by the Sea: A Global Conference:* "Niagara Overlook" (winner of the Poetry by the Sea Sonnet Contest)

Rattle: "On Looking at an MRI Cross-Section," "Marooned," "Caught in the Webb"

Snakeskin: "The Martian Anthropologist Weighs In"

The Washington Post Style Invitational: "Exit Pall"

SATAN TALKS TO
HIS THERAPIST

On Looking at an MRI Cross-Section

actual photo below

Inside my head, I learn, a horseshoe crab
stares heavenward with jumbo-olive eyes
(the pitted kind), each in an ice cream cone
webbed like a goose's foot. Between them flies
bright looping wire.
And past each ice cream cone, a marbled slab
of glossy, skinless chicken-off-the-bone
spreads like a wing. Behind the meat and flab?
A gown for those who like their skirts outsize
and half on fire.

So this is it: from fruit to flaming dress
hums every memory I've kept since birth—
each love and hate, each lesson I've been taught
and not ejected,
each town, café, or weedy patch of earth,
each brilliant scheme or idiotic thought.
In other words, it's just the sort of mess
I'd have expected.

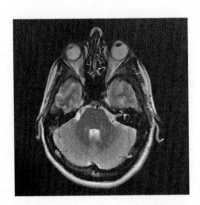

SPIRALING
DOWN

Marooned

Nothing moves us like a person stuck—
a toddler in a well, a stranded scout:
we gather at our screens and pray for luck.

Will storms bypass the climbers? Run amok?
Will all those boaters perish like beached trout?
Nothing moves us like a person stuck,

a coach trapped with his soccer team, their pluck
despite the odds, the rising tide of doubt;
we mourn a diver who ran out of luck

and hold our breath while others roll and tuck
through limestone passages to get them out.
Nothing moves us like a person stuck—

except for seeing (teary, thunderstruck)
the things we've longed for finally come about:
rescues soaked in undiluted luck.

And then we're back to making our next buck,
to swimming after consequence and clout.
Nothing moves us. Like a person stuck,
we peer from caves of bone and pray for luck.

Thanksgiving Climate Change Song

*(to the tune of "Over the River
and Through the Woods")*

Over the river and through the woods
To Grandma's we planned to go,
But floods rose all day
And the bridge washed away
And a Honda is hard to row.

Over to Amtrak we went, of course,
Which would have been just fine
If wildfires had not
Occurred on the spot
To block the 4:09.

Over our budget, we caught a plane—
We'd soon take off, we knew!
But cyclones and swarms
Of tropical storms
Had stranded the whole damn crew.

Over and over we tried to Zoom:
Hail knocked the power dead.
No time to stay put,
We've departed on foot
For New Year's Eve instead.

Melissa Balmain

Fatal Mistakes

The pill you're sure is good for you,
the mole you think you can neglect,
the ache you blame on winter flu:
it's always what you least expect.

The mat that pads your shower floor,
the flight you take from home, direct,
the car that's never stalled before:
it's always what you least expect.

The oddly coiffed New York tycoon
whom no one ever would elect
because he's nutty as a loon . . .
it's always what you least expect.

Wednesday in Mount Hope Cemetery

"The modest grave site of suffrage icon
Susan B. Anthony, now a shrine to women's rights,
is drawing overflow crowds Tuesday as voters
consider choosing the nation's first female president."
—[Rochester] *Democrat & Chronicle*,
November 8, 2016

Woken yesterday by all those feet,
I felt—at last!—like grinning.
Today: few visitors. A quiet street.
And news that has me spinning.

Melissa Balmain

Fruit and Consequences

When a bruise on an apple is almost not there—
a diminutive, delicate, decorous blip
scarcely bigger around than a baby flea's hair—

it becomes the one part our attention can't skip;
though the rest of the fruit is as smooth as good booze,
we will pass it right up with a curl of the lip.

But suppose that an apple's got bruise upon bruise,
toxic mold that would make a mycologist squirm,
and a core full of rot that is starting to ooze:

we'll keep searching the thing from its stem to its worm
for a spot—any spot!—that our stomachs can bear,
then elect that bad apple to serve its first term.

Breaking

Watching our children at the beach,
we ought to smile and schmooze,
but—phones regrettably in reach—
we're swamped by waves of news:

A crook goes free. A mouthpiece quits.
More leaders mix with commies.
Each hour or so, the Prez emits
a couple tweet tsunamis.

Battered and weary on the shore,
we fight for breath and wonder
how many more can hit before
they finally drag us under.

Melissa Balmain

Dorothy Parker's Ghost Weighs in on the "New Political Climate"

Men get free passes
For grabbing girls' asses.

Five Ages of Woman

I

I howl like a brute
and befoul my pink suit
but the grownups declare that I'm dainty
and cute.

II

Though all of the boys
are allowed to make noise
I am told to exhibit politeness
and poise.

III

Nine times out of ten
I am listened to when
my ideas are echoed more loudly
by men.

IV

Chauffeuring my kid
I do just as I'm bid—
stay unseen, my opinions kept under
a lid.

V

I gum pureed fruit
and regret I can't shoot
all the nursing home staffers who murmur
I'm cute.

Melissa Balmain

In the Beeswax Room

for Gina Ingoglia Weiner (1938–2015)

"The Laib Wax Room, lined with fragrant beeswax
and illuminated by a single bare light bulb, is the first
permanently installed artwork at the Phillips since the
Rothko Room in 1960."
　—The Phillips Collection

Within these golden walls, this honey scent,
no anxious question makes my head go numb,
no frantic, topsy-turvy argument.
The sound, the only sound, is my blood's hum.

In here your latest awful news can't come:
my purse was confiscated lest it dent
the wax—and with it went my phone. In sum,
within these golden walls, this honey scent,

my brain flies back to all the hours you spent
in kitchen glow, pale crust beneath your thumb,
me watching from below, impressed, content
(no anxious question makes my head go numb);

I see you, candle-lit, at meals while dumb
debates flared. (Neither sibling would relent
till you leaned in and shushed us with aplomb.)
No, frantic, topsy-turvy argument

was *my* thing then, before the cosmos bent
and your idea of lunch became a crumb,
your stifled groans an hourly event,
the sound the only sound.
　　　　　　　　Is my blood's hum

the same as yours, still half-remembered from
another room, my first?
                              The light just went.
It's closing time. My heart begins to drum.
If only there were space that I could rent
within these golden walls.

Melissa Balmain

To Mom, in the Beyond

Two candles and three photos had to stand
atop the bureau that I used each summer.
No space for me to stack some books? *Quelle bummer.*
Each mantelpiece and shelf was also planned,
each ledge, nook, countertop, bare inch of floor,
or wedge of open air beneath a gable.
Even the sill behind the ping-pong table—
those poor doomed tchotchkes!—was accounted for.
Oh, how your decorating drove us nuts
(as tasteful as it was), your certainty
that everybody knew it would behoove them
to raise no disrespectful ifs or buts,
and leave each bud vase, bowl, or bottle be.
They're all still there, of course: we'd hate to move them.

We Make the Mask

Spring 2020
(with apologies to Paul Laurence Dunbar)

We make the mask that shields and ties,
Unclear about the hows or whys:
Bandanas work, says Surgeon G.,
While others cry, *Tomfoolery!*
Plus, there's debate regarding plies—

How many layers will paralyze
Those droplets of a certain size,
Yet leave good breathability?
We make the mask

Again, again, as we surmise
Which tips to cherish or despise.
Will all this save us? Or have we
Just saved the craft economy
With fabric, thread and ribbon buys
            To make the mask?

Melissa Balmain

Contingency Plan

If I come down with it and don't recover,
I hope you'll find yourself another lover—
somebody smart and kind and never rowdy
whose inner weather isn't ever cloudy,
who cooks as if she sprang from Julia Child
and sings so sweetly, thrushes are beguiled,
who doesn't make you fix the lamps and plumbing
or clean for guests you'd rather weren't coming,
who finds your point of view completely valid
re: eating Oreos instead of salad,
who reads the same archaic tomes that you do
and likes to pair them with erotic voodoo . . .
in other words, your dream girl to the letter—
except she looks just like an Irish setter.

Coronostalgia

The dream where I'm taking a midterm
for a class that, I realize with fright,
I can't name or recall having been to at all?
I'd be tickled to dream it tonight.

The one where I'm topless in public—
or, more often than not, naked-assed—
and encounter my boss? What a terrible loss
that this dream is a thing of the past.

Hey—even the one where I'm driving,
though I'm half in the rear middle seat,
and I notice (say what?) that my eyes are glued shut,
has become an impossible treat.

Instead, I keep having a nightmare
my poor nerves can no longer withstand,
one that loops without end: I wave hi to a friend
who runs up and *starts shaking my hand*.

Melissa Balmain

Sidewalk Face-Off

Look! From opposite directions,
wearing masks to thwart infections,
two athletic pairs of spouses
march past neo-Tudor houses.
Sneakers pound and pulses quicken:
it's a game of COVID-chicken!

Who will keep on striding forward,
chin and eyeballs firmly lowered?
Who will scurry six feet over
to the dog-doo-studded clover,
fearful that they'll later sicken
thanks to playing COVID-chicken?

Every day the teams assemble.
Every day their innards tremble
like the innards of scared rabbits,
but they keep their walking habits:
in a world that's stalled and stricken
there's no sport but COVID-chicken.

Satan Talks to His Therapist

Fall 2020

I've had four perfect years planned out for *ages*:

Split families up and stick the brats in cages;
dump cherished friendships in a flaming pool;
give power only to the dumb or cruel
and money just to those who have too much.

Let wholesome standards wither at my touch;
get better at exterminating birds
and swapping forests out for cattle herds;
befoul each breath of air and gulp of water.

Grant every mother, girlfriend, wife or daughter
the same respect as parasitic worms;
rouse bigots (in amusing coded terms)
while keeping them supplied with Colts and Glocks.

Where there's a henhouse, guard it with a Fox;
spawn loopholes, larceny and legalese;
and best of all, when there's a new disease,
make sure fantastic numbers will be killed . . .

And yet (life isn't fair!) I'm unfulfilled.
Each time I try to carry out a plan,
I'm beaten to it by that blasted *man*.
Each yummy lie I long to spread? He's spread it.

At least some people give me all the credit.

Melissa Balmain

My Thoughts and Prayers Go Out to You

Well, of course your mom was precious and I'm sad
    she's not alive,
but the answer's not to confiscate my HK MP5—
it's to hand all moms their own! You'd still be
    Mama's honeybun
if, instead of brunch on Mother's Day, you'd thought
    to give a gun,
give a gun, give a gun, give a love-your-mama gun.

As for spouses, yours was beautiful before her head blew off—
how I wish you'd bought yourselves a his-and-hers
    Kalashnikov,
and avoided parties, films and other useless couples' fun.
Friday night's for weapons training, it's a chance to date a gun,
date a gun, date a gun, date a hot-o-matic gun.

And your little boy? Adorable—a shame he couldn't bolt.
He's our proof that every teacher ought to have the latest Colt,
plus a practice range where tire swings and tetherballs
    once spun.
Skip those silly games at recess till each Teach can aim a gun,
aim a gun, aim a gun, aim a Core-required gun.

So come on, quit being haters, don't you give my rights
    a shove.
There's a way for me to keep my gun, and you the folks
    you love!
All it takes is recognition that your highest goal, bar none,
is to plan your daily lives around my need to own a gun
that is deadlier than any used from Vicksburg to Verdun,
while ensuring that this right belongs to nearly everyone,

even online-shopping crazies who buy rifles by the ton.
Love my gun, love my gun—you're the planets, it's the sun.
Love my gun, love my gun: if you don't, you'd better run.

Melissa Balmain

Uncombable

"US boy with uncombable hair syndrome becomes
Instagram hit"
—*The Guardian*

Uncombable hair? Well, of course it's a thing:
we've arrived in uncombable times
with uncombable dangers, uncombable ills,
and uncombable thought paradigms.

Nuts with guns are uncombable (so we've been told)—
we are doomed to uncombable grief.
Piles of nukes are uncombable; superbugs too,
and decay in the Barrier Reef.

Our hatreds? Uncombable. Ditto our loves
of red meat, SUVs, fossil fuel,
and the systems permitting too few of our kids
to be nourished and housed and in school.

Yes, it's all so uncombable: that's what we'll hear
as we fall and the rising sea foams—
unless our uncombable powers that be
can agree on some *new* fucking combs.

The Upside of Grief

It levers you open. It wakes you.
You're attentive, alert and aware.
Hocus-pocus, the world snaps in focus
from the grass to the geese in the air.

Every cantaloupe sunset unmakes you,
every sniff of a rose or pot pie;
a warm kitten, a muffin you've bitten
has you suddenly dabbing your eye

as the thought of *last time* overtakes you—
back before swift events could destroy
any glimmer of hope, then get grimmer.
(To be honest? You'd still prefer joy.)

Melissa Balmain

IN LIMBO

Caught in the Webb

"If you held a grain of sand up to the sky at arm's length,
that tiny speck is the size of Webb's view in this image.
Imagine—galaxies galore within a grain . . ."
         —NASA Webb Telescope's Twitter account

My morning newsfeed teems with shots of space—
bright slopes and swirls of russet and vermilion
that shelter hidden planets by the billion.
Soon, soon my puny brain will try to face
the likelihood that everything I do
is just a blip of no more real importance
than goings-on atop that speck of Horton's
in Dr. Seuss's book; that I'm a Who,
and there's no god who gives a flip for me
or anybody else as we're revolving
among the other galaxies that hurtle,
all dreaming, planning, acting pointlessly.
Soon, soon I'll face this—once I finish solving
(*ta-da! I did it!*) Spelling Bee and Wordle.

Preposterous

> "It's time to preorder your Thanksgiving turkey"
> —Sign spotted outside a butcher shop in September

It's never too soon to preorder that turkey,
to pre-splurge on lights and white pine
for Christmas and New Year's
(not one year's, but two years'!),
to pre-pour the Valentine's wine.

So pre-April-Fool 'em! Pre-launch July rockets!
Pre-charbroil that Labor Day cow!
Don't waste precious minutes
on days that you're *in*: it's
too late to be having fun now.

Melissa Balmain

The Martian Anthropologist Weighs In

After Craig Raine

They pick it up each time it cries—
the tiny creature calms right down—
and tickle it from foot to crown
or murmur doting lullabies.

It travels with them everywhere,
indoors and out, at home, on trips,
pressed snugly to their breasts or hips.
(If it got lost, they'd have a scare!)

By day, its face keeps them beguiled.
By night, they seldom sleep apart.
Oh, how it animates my heart
to see these humans with a child—

until it's one or maybe two,
and then, of course, you know the score:
they take it to the Apple Store
to trade it in for someone new.

"William Shakespeare (@ShakespeareWi) is now following you on Twitter!"

(actual Twitter notification)

He's back—of course he is! I should have known.
What artist of his stature could resist
a chance to fret about the Eurozone
and mill our century's dramatic grist?
I eagerly look up his latest tweet,
expecting links to *Will and Kate, Part II*
and *Summer's Tale, or Climate Change Compleat* . . .
but find—uh oh—mere quotes from *Much Ado.*
Sighing, I track him down on Instagram
and Snapchat, where he does his daily duty
of sharing memes—"'Tis Hamlet made of ham!"—
and praising "Dame Kardashian's beauteous booty";
then Facebook, where he likes a dancing kitten,
and posts, "Alack! Why can't I get more written?"

Melissa Balmain

Blue-Plate Special

Washington, D.C., December 2019 and January 2021

It sounds so delicious—*mmm, peach-mint*—
a dish of fruit, sugar and flour
that arrives piping hot, topped with cognac (a lot),
and takes minutes to make and devour.

But instead the thing's bitter and tricky
(the recipe's centuries old),
an impossible meal—a soufflé stuffed with eel—
that of course we'll be serving ice cold.

Will the one that it's for duly eat it?
Will he vomit it up on our shirts?
Who among us can say? All that's left is to pray
that in time there will be just desserts.

Exit Pall

Midterm votes are done:
optimism's fading fast
that the folks who won
somehow will—unlike the last—
see that more than gas gets passed.

Melissa Balmain

Tit for Tat: One-Syll Tips for Pols

> "Have you ever noticed that most politicians
> speak in remarkably simplified plain language?
> This is intentional, with most communicating
> far below their educational achievements and
> speaking somewhere around a fourth grade
> level, and sometimes a bit higher. The idea is to
> make concepts simple, with the message easy to
> understand, easy to remember, and easy to digest."
> —OS X Daily

Don't drop your pants and aim your phone,
tell lies re how much cash you've blown,
let wing nuts treat you like their pup,
get names of heads of state mixed up,
say dumb, mean stuff when mics are on,
give jobs to pals, or toke till dawn.
(But will you heed? We know you won't.
Could be the word you miss is "don't.")

Invasive Species
(Or: Overheard on a Cruise Ship)

> "Scientists and conservationists agree that introduced
> plants and animals represent the single greatest threat to
> the terrestrial ecosystems of Galápagos."
> —Galápagos Conservancy

"The goats are just a menace, so I hear,
devouring shrubbery like some John Deere
and leaving nothing for the giant tortoise.
Poor thing ends up with early rigor mortis.

"Pet cats? Now there's a never-ending mess.
It seems they can't be satisfied unless
they stuff themselves each time they come upon a
young lava lizard or marine iguana . . .

"But worst of all is the *philornis* fly.
Its larvae lurk in nests, suck chicks half dry,
deform their beaks and sap their strength by inches,
until it's *adiós* to Darwin's finches.

"Those islands are all doomed, I would expect.
Thank God we're visiting before they're wrecked—
two hundred thousand tourists just this year!
The restaurants are charming, so I hear."

Melissa Balmain

To the Blue Jay That Woke Me Every Morning—
Until the Day I Leaned Out My Window and Roared,
and It Flew Away in a Panic

That day

If only your voice were a fraction as pretty
as your tail and your back and your crest,
I'd have gratefully welcomed your daily dawn ditty
and sprung from my bed to get dressed.

But instead your high-decibel, rusty-hinge squawk
is as far as could be from life's joys—
it's like seeing Fran Drescher, then hearing her talk:
how could beauty be paired with such noise?

Sixteen years later

During strolls ever since, I've spied robins aplenty,
scarlet tanagers, cardinals too,
and some species that even surprise cognoscenti,
but seldom your wonderful blue.

Paranoia? Perhaps, but I'll venture a stab:
you alerted your friends all around
to steer clear of a beast, feathers droopy and drab,
that makes the world's ghastliest sound.

Thumbelina Moves On

Who cares if I was born inside a flower
and you're the only Flower Fairy Prince?
We marveled at these facts for half an hour,
but haven't had a conversation since.
Relationships, it's clear, need stronger glue
than such a superficial parallel,
or than the boring truth that, just like you,
I'd fit in an abandoned peanut shell.
So, sorry, Prince: like Bluebird, Mole and Toad,
you won't be making me your little bride—
it's time for more adventures on the road!
(I'm pretty sure that I can thumb a ride.)

Melissa Balmain

Morning Report

for Bill

Again you dreamed of flying,
plus swimming in the deep
with humpback whales you saved from dying
before you had to leap

ashore—a tête-à-tête in
Beijing required your clout,
so diplomats (Chinese, Tibetan)
could finally work things out.

And me, you ask? As always,
my dreams were super too.
I wandered roach-infested hallways,
contracted avian flu,

then landed someplace—Hades?—
with men's rooms near and far,
but not a single door marked "Ladies"
(I had to use a jar).

Tonight, love, I'll be ready:
Before I snore and drool,
I plan to picture something heady—
the ocean, green and cool—

so that (asleep) I'll paddle
where I can watch you pass
astride your humpback's golden saddle,
and spear you in the ass.

Niagara Overlook

for Davey at 16

As you gaze at the falls, unaware that I'm there,
I survey your brow's drop-off, the bluff of your chin,
and the stone that bobs high in your neck, sharp and thin;
the bright eddies and riffles that play in the hair
that meanders from temple to earlobe to nape;
and above all, your eyes, squinting hard at the view,
eyes I've known since before their transparent spring blue
silted over (your grandfather's color, dad's shape).
What desires are cascading behind that gaze now?
What inventions are coursing right up to your brink?
How I wish I could ask and go barreling deep—
but of course that's too much for a boy to allow.
So I'll stay where I am, far away from the drink,
in the hope that one day you'll invite me to leap.

Melissa Balmain

To My Son, Upon Removal of One of My Ovaries

"I wish I knew which one I was from."
—Davey, age 20

Was it lefty or righty that started you out
(with some help, naturally, from your dad)?
Who can tell? All I know is I've got to let go
of your earliest bachelor pad—

helpful practice, perhaps, for a time soon to come
when you'll seldom spend weeks, even days,
in the blue, boyhood room where the '80s tunes boom
and you sleep until noon on vacays;

when I'll travel to see the apartment you've found
in Manhattan's or Silicon's dregs,
and I'll pray till I burst that at least—like your first—
your new neighborhood has some good eggs.

Being the parent . . .

       . . . means, at family meals,
you pour and ladle while your food congeals,
then eat the Brussels sprouts the children spurned
because they're burned,
the chicken leg with unattractive gore,
the slice of sourdough that hit the floor.
And if there's not enough dessert for each,
you grab a peach,
as stoic as Ma Joad,
while they have brownies à la mode.

It means when there's a spider in the john
so big it ought to have a collar on,
and you would rather opt for spidercide
or simply hide,
you have to show them how to trap the thing
inside a glass, then nonchalantly bring
it out of doors where it can leap and land
as nature planned,
before you stride back in
to find it clinging to your shin.

It means the movies, plays and TV shows
you watch are ones another person chose.
It means you have no privacy. It means
no spicy greens
or stinky cheese or fish that's on the bone.
And when at last the kids have up and flown
and you're allowed to do just as you please,
from bugs to bries,
it means this change you thought
would help you miss them less does not.

                        Melissa Balmain

What Dylan Thomas Would Say if He Were Around for National Donut Day

Donut, go gentle into that good night:
In middle-age, I beg you, stay away.
I can't afford to take another bite.

Although you've helped to keep my outlook bright
(Along with HBO and chardonnay),
Donut, go gentle into that good night,

Whether you're jelly, glazed or filled with white;
From diner, bakery or swank café
I can't afford. To take another bite

Is all I hunger for when you're in sight,
Despite the heavy price you make me pay.
Donut, go gentle into that good night

Or my circumference will match my height
And I'll have acne till my dying day.
I can't afford to take another bite,

Not even on the road—wait, hang a right!
Curse, bless you, Krispy Kreme, soft as soufflé!
Donut, go gentle into that good night?
I can't afford . . . ? OK, I'll have a bite.

Memo to Self, in Middle Age

Go ahead: pump up your lips
with flab you siphon from your hips,
sand down those cheeks, syringe that chin
and neck with quarts of collagen,
drown every hair in L'Oréal,
balloon both boobs with MemoryGel
till your reflection swears to you
you're not a day past thirty-two—
feel free! But though the glass pretends,
beware of gazing at old friends
who haven't masked their age a bit:
they'll do the job your mirror quit.

Melissa Balmain

Fallen

As a kid growing up in New York,
I considered our fall second rate:
how I longed for the grand, mythological land
we exotically labeled *Upstate.*

In that Eden, I'd heard, leaves turned bright,
endless acres of yellows and reds,
while my single tree browned, dropping one tiny mound
that I kicked to the curb with my Keds.

Now I live several hours to the north,
and the maples and oaks truly blaze—
hues so loud they look fake—till the time comes to rake
without stopping, for numberless days.

And I daydream of trips farther south,
of the places I'll shop, stroll and dine
in that part of the map where the leaves may be crap
but you don't need a rod in your spine.

To-Do

Someday I'll do it: straighten all my closets
and purge those vests from 1993,
scrub tile and grout of mineral deposits,
arrange my spices alphabetically.
I'll find the puzzle pieces that need finding,
repair my Penguin classics, page and binding,
then polish every doorknob till it's blinding.

My photographs? At last I'll organize them.
My shrubbery? I'll finally cut it back.
I'll wax the table scratches to disguise them,
hang every poster, painting, pennant, plaque.
I'll give my rhododendrons hits of acid,
file pamphlets on lakes Tupper, George and Placid,
re-stuff each quilt and pillow that's gone flaccid.

And when I've done it all—when, to perfection,
I've finished off the items on my list,
when not a speck of dust awaits detection,
and not a squeaky door hinge has been missed,
and not a scrapbook scrap remains unpasted,
and not a seam's un-finished or un-basted,
I'll die, my final year completely wasted.

Melissa Balmain

Native Fauna

"Wildlife roams as the planet's human population isolates"
—ABC News, Spring 2020

Dolphins near Turkey and turkeys in Pittsburgh
and foxes on Washington's Mall
may be having a ball—
but their numbers would pall next to what's in my hall
and beneath all my chairs,
and in pairs on my stairs,
having fuzzy affairs:
herds of dust bunnies, thriving as nature intends.

Monkeys in India, pumas in Chile,
and pelicans swarming Peru
may be awesome to view,
but there's little they do that my bunnies can't too—
cling and swing way up high,
curl and stretch, or just lie,
and at times even fly . . .
yes, a dust bunny's versatile day never ends.

Nobody visits me in the pandemic,
so why should I bother to clean
till we get a vaccine?
Why not reign as the queen of the dust bunny scene?
And another big win:
just consider what's *in*
all these bunnies—hair, skin!
They're the closest I come now to making new friends.

The Test

Before

My stomach feels sick
at the size of her stick.

During

Anxiety grows
as she roots in my nose.

After

Forget all the minuses:
I've now got clean sinuses.

Melissa Balmain

When the Chips Are Down . . .

Is your pulsating earache a thing-you-should-fear ache?
Could tumors be lodged in your brain?
Do you let this one slide or risk taking a ride
to a clinic? Your choice becomes plain:
you'll stay in, drink some gin, picture numbers that spin,
place your bet . . .
and start playing pandemic roulette.

Now your cat's acting grumpy, and smells like some lump he
coughed up on the living room floor—
should you grab him and go for a checkup, or no?
You decide that you'll have to ignore
the new whir in his purr and the mats in his fur,
skip the vet,
and keep playing pandemic roulette.

Plus of course there's your toddler, that balance-free waddler,
and clumsy, impetuous spouse:
when they topple and bleed, is a pro what they need?
Nah, you'll stitch them up right in the house,
getting by, while they cry, with some tips from a guy
on the Net,
since you're playing pandemic roulette.

It's the closest to Vegas you'll come in this plague, as
you gamble no torment or ill
(that you'd normally shout to a doctor about)
will deform or disable or kill
while you wait and you wait for that mythical date
when the threat
is no sweat

and you'll get—
you hope yet!—
to quit playing pandemic roulette.

Melissa Balmain

"Coffee Drinking Linked to Lower Mortality Risk, New Study Finds"

—The New York Times

Alas, though the headline is earnestly meant,
our mortality risk's still 100 percent.

CLIMBING
OUT

Best in Show

"So is it like the Westminster Kennel Club,
but with poems?"

—A friend, after hearing that I was
judging a poetry contest

Here are the poems that wag a great tale;
that ripple with muscular verbs;
the light ones, the dark ones,
the bound-through-the-park ones;
the ones that go sniffing at curbs.

Here is the sonnet with well-bred allusions;
the triolet ready to beg
with its soft friendly pause
and manicured clause;
the limerick humping your leg.

Oh, how you long to give treats to them all
(even the poems that bite,
or force you to look as
they lick their own tuchus)
to keep them from howling all night.

But of course only one gets to fetch the big trophy,
so you comb and you vet till you know,
in a month and an age,
that a lone dog-eared page
has jumped in your lap and won't go.

Treasure Map

for X.J. Kennedy,
approaching his ninetieth birthday

X marks the spot where wit is found,
where puckish turns of phrase abound,
allowing readers—ill, in debt,
or stuck with Fluffy at the vet—
to have their sorrows so well drowned,
      their socks get wet.

X designates the sacred ground
upon which ballads might resound
so crisply (like a fresh baguette!)
and smoothly (like a Gulfstream jet!)
they'll later work their way around
      the Internet.

Behind it all? A soul renowned
for charm and patience that astound;
for shrewd critiques that make us sweat;
for kindness that, it's safe to bet,
one day will get him winged and gowned—
      but please, not yet.

Melissa Balmain

Understatement

for Rhina P. Espaillat
on her ninetieth birthday

She's a writing machine, a
bicultural queen, a
savant from sestina
to forms much more lean. A
machete's not keen, a
macaw is dull green, a
Swiss Alp's a ravine, a
cold brew lacks caffeine, a
soufflé's junk cuisine—ah,
   compared to the bite
   and the color (so bright!)
   and the eloquent height
   and the buzz (through the night!)
   and the tasty delight
of a poem by Rhina.

Getting Spammed by Wendy Cope's Hacked Email Account

(with apologies to W.C. and Kingsley A.)

It happened to me yesterday—
A pretty boring story,
But still the closest I've come in months
To literary glory.

Melissa Balmain

Public Relations

In my forties, I learned to like coffee.
In my fifties, I've taken up drink.
In my sixties, what vice will begin to seem nice?
It's pretty exciting to think.

Cigarettes? Corncob pipes? Chaw and Juul pods?
By my seventies, surely a bong.
And by eighty, you know that wherever I go,
I'll bring a few uppers along.

By the time I hit ninety, I'm hopeful
those who pegged me as square and old school
will take note of my slide and at last will decide,
Let's read that great-grandma—she's cool.

Supermoon

Six days after a presidential election

> "The brightest supermoon in almost 70 years
> rises tonight."
>> —*LA Times*, November 13, 2016

The brightest yet, the experts cried;
thank God we'd lived to see her glide,
to celebrate this night, this show.
Eager to gape from far below,
we wolfed our dinner, trooped outside.

But where was the triumphant ride?
Surely those experts hadn't lied . . .
In dumb alarm, we watched as, whoa,
the brightest yet

became completely mummified
by gas and vapor, deep and wide.
We told ourselves she still might glow;
the truth, we saw at last, was no.
Who would have guessed dark clouds could hide
the brightest yet?

Years later, with the #MeToo movement in full swing

> "A supermoon's extra pull of gravity creates
> higher-than-usual tides."
>> —earthsky.org

Was it the moon? We'll never know
what force—precipitous or slow,
coincidental or applied—
emerged at last to turn the tide
and roil the secret status quo.

Melissa Balmain

Whatever caused this epic flow,
as it recedes, the heaps will grow:
bottom dwellers—wrinkled, dried.
Was it the moon

that beached the eels who used to go
in search of mermaids, even though
the mermaids often fled (or tried)?
Now every day more eels are fried
and served up with our morning joe.
Was it the moon?

Zoom Recital: Gallery View

A little dancer tiptoes on her lawn.
In kitchens, other girls and moms look on.

The dancer leaps and lands on her caboose.
One mom jumps up, serves sandwiches and juice.

Next kid attempts a not-so-grand plié.
Mom 2 squats deeply, putting pots away.

Another girl sashays, confused, and stops . . .
With speedy sideways strokes, Mom 3 dry-mops . . .

. . . performs a half-arched, wobbly arabesque . . .
. . . curves gracefully a moment by her desk . . .

. . . before she drops into a painful split.
. . . then turns to bake and boil, no time to sit.

The dancers bow. They clap for all the others.
Someday (who knows?) they might applaud their mothers.

Melissa Balmain

Moonshine

"Many scientists have historically believed Earth's
large moon was generated by a collision between
proto-Earth . . . and a large, Mars-sized impactor. . . .
In order to find out whether other planets can
form similarly large moons, [scientists] conducted
impact simulations on the computer . . ."
—The University of Rochester's Newscenter

Parents, of course, are smirking at this test.
We need no laboratory simulation
to tell us if a hot collision's best
for rapid and reliable creation
of something molten that solidifies
and grows so fast our reason can't absorb it,
that's soon a body of sufficient size
to show itself and wrap us in its orbit.
Nor do we need a scientist to run
a study seeing if this satellite
has greater claims than we do on the sun—
as much as we pretend our future's bright,
one certainty inevitably grips us:
our purpose is to help the kid eclipse us.

Bubble Rap

Inspired by real events in 1977

Jeannie and Jill had shiny hair—
Parted, down-to-their-heinie hair,
And perfect clogs and bell-bottom cords,
And abdomens as flat as boards,
And dangly earrings and endless supplies
Of friends to go out with for Burger King fries.
And on her birthday—I was struck dumb!—
Jill got a house made of Bubble Yum.

A Bubble Yum house. A Bubble Yum house.
A stacks-of-packs-of-Bubble-Yum house.

Jeannie had built it; it was 12 inches high.
Jill brought it to school so we all could sigh.
Even our teacher, Mrs. Zabel,
Admired each Grape and Original gable.
Later that day on the playground grass
Jill divvied up the house with half our class
While the rest of us stood there, feeling glum
'Cause we didn't rate a pack of Bubble Yum.

A Bubble Yum house. A Bubble Yum house.
Jill flaunted, I wanted, a Bubble Yum house.

My hair was too short and my pants too long;
No clogs for me (Mom's aversion was strong—
Same deal with earrings) and I wasn't blessed
With abs even half as flat as my chest.
Burger King fries? They were allowed,
But I wasn't part of the popular crowd.

Melissa Balmain

So I saved my allowance, every crumb,
To buy me a heap of Bubble Yum.

A Bubble Yum house. A Bubble Yum house.
I'd be cool as a pool with a Bubble Yum house.

The weeks crept by; at the corner store
I bought 10 packs, then 10 packs more:
I was getting close, despite '70s inflation,
To tasty walls and a sweet foundation.
When I bragged to a buddy, she stared at her shoes:
Hadn't I heard the latest news?
Nobody cool still chewed that gum—
There were spider eggs in Bubble Yum.

A Bubble Yum house. A Bubble Yum house.
No preteen could be seen with a Bubble Yum house.

O cruel fate! Though riddled with doubt,
I threw every pack of my Bubble Yum out—
Just before the claims of spider eggs
Were proven to have zero legs.
The decades flew. Can't chew gum today
If I don't want to aggravate my TMJ,
And yet . . . now and then, I still succumb
To visions of a house of Bubble Yum.

A Bubble Yum house. A Bubble Yum house.
A double-yum, no-trouble-yum, Bubble Yum house.
When I die, I expect my kids and spouse
To bury me in a Bubble Yum house.

A Japanese Maple Grows in Brooklyn

> "With maturity, the bonsai slowly comes into harmony,
> believing it is a 30-foot-tall tree in the landscape."
> —Sign at the Brooklyn Botanic Garden

Sapling

I've read that sign—a bunch of bunk.
What bonsai thinks it's ten yards high?
The people who tend my twigs and trunk
are several times as tall as I.
Trapped in this pot, my prospects shrunk,
if I were a weeping cherry, I'd cry.

Mature Tree

The people who tend my twigs and trunk?
For decades I've seen them smile and sigh
as I've sat here like a Shingon monk
and they've flourished, faded, and passed by.
At last I know—who would've thunk?—
that compared to them, I brush the sky.

Melissa Balmain

My Mother's Ghost Whispers in My Ear at Starbucks

You always skip the cream and go with skim:
"Why guzzle all those extra calories?"
Determined to be healthy—hard and slim—
you always skip the cream and go with skim.
I went with cheese and butter, skipped the gym,
and died too early due to none of these.
You always skip the cream and go with skim—
why? Guzzle all those extra calories.

A Literal-Minded Virgin Reads Robert Herrick

"Gather ye rosebuds"? If I may,
Who's got the time to garden?
To plant and prune the day away
While all my arteries harden?

As for the so-called lamp above,
Damn straight it's getting higher!
No sunscreen, hat, or canvas glove
Can save me from that fryer.

It's clear, from everything you've said,
You're with some yardwork lobby
That thinks a gal who's still unwed
Should pick this stupid hobby.

Screw that. I'll spend a little dough
And save my health and hours.
When I want rosebuds, I'll just go
To 1-800-FLOWERS.

Melissa Balmain

The Sheltering Suburbanite
to Her Neighbor

> "Many families are now grappling with whether, when
> and how to open their pandemic-quarantine bubbles to
> additional people."
> —*The Wall Street Journal*

(sorry, Christopher Marlowe)

Come live with me inside my bubble:
Our cozy and exclusive club'll
Share real—not Zoomed or FaceTimed!—meals,
Plus, if the ease of it appeals,

We'll work around supply-chain glitches
By pooling all our greatest riches:
My yeast can now be yours as well,
My Charmin, Clorox and Purell.

And we'll take walks, no longer shouting
The way we had to when each outing
Meant trying for a heart-to-heart
While eardrums struggled yards apart.

And I'll divide my sourdough starter,
And you will generously barter
Your sewing skills. (I'd love a cute
New mask and tailored hazmat suit.)

It just makes sense that we should weather
This crisis (cautiously) together!
Now free at last to hug hello,
We'll meet each day for morning joe;

We'll gossip while our kids are playing;
I'll paint your nails . . . What's that you're saying?
A nail salon? You went at 3?
Stay the fuck away from me.

Melissa Balmain

Philip Larkin Tries for a Vaccine Appointment

Another long computer sesh
As I attempt to land a day
Before the bloody end of May:
Log in, refresh, refresh, refresh . . .

Vaxxed Life

It's just as I dreamed! Thanks to vials from Pfizer
      I'm off to reunions with people I've missed—
first the dentist (could I have a fractured incisor?),
      a physical therapist (what's with my wrist?),
ophthalmologist (how come my eyeballs are aching?),
      podiatrist (will all my toenails fall off?),
cardiologist (why am I dizzy when waking?)
      and allergist (is this a terminal cough?).
After that, who can tell which new doctors will vet me
      or what they'll vet *for*: deadly clot? Toxic sting?
What a privilege it is, now that COVID won't get me,
      to worry again about every damn thing.

Melissa Balmain

For My Mother-in-Law, Trapped in Her Nursing Home by Another Viral Outbreak

After A.E. Housman

Loneliest of trees, a cherry blooms
Unseen by you whose spartan rooms
Have windows that are far too high
For views of anything but sky.

Now with your nineties in full swing,
You've doubtless started wondering
If last year's rides to see spring's glory
Were the last ones in your story.

And so you're gamely making do
With what's available to you:
A faded sprig from Mother's Day;
Pink sneakers; blushing fruit puree.

Undergrowth

The worst part of spring isn't pollen,
or sickly and trickly catarrh,
or the slippery petals soon fallen
on patio, driveway and car.
I can live with the rains always plinking,
black mud and brown crud on my Keds,
and the hailstorms that, just when I'm thinking,
"Nice tulips!" come bomb them to shreds.

No, the horror of spring is recession:
when snow starts to go, the world's peeled;
April warmth brings an end to discretion
as tufts, long unmown, lie revealed.
I can feel myself blushing—will neighbors
catch sight of this blight, winter's dregs,
and be shocked at my slackening labors?
I sigh, and I go shave my legs.

Melissa Balmain

Jingle for a Law Firm

> "No rhymes. Just results."
>> —Law firm ad spotted on a New York billboard,
>> in response to the rhyming ads of rival firms

Hurt at work or in a car?
Call Farr, Barr, Starr and Henderson.

That's 888-8888!
Our legal team is truly fine.

We're grads of NYU and Yale;
We make our cases without snags—

And till we win (you know we will),
You won't receive a single charge.

So hire us! You can't go wrong!
Just don't forget this catchy tune.

To My Husband, Re My Tennis Elbow

I never had it, back when I played tennis,
despite those twisting forehands, serves and lobs,
but now a heavy bag or some such menace
has brought it on—and as the tendon throbs,

I lie awake and think, Could this be karma?
A punishment for dropping racquet sports?
Are armbands and dependence on Big Pharma
part of a sentence by the cosmic courts

for squandering my years of youthful practice,
of hamstrings, gluteals and deltoids flexed?
And now a thought as spiky as a cactus:
What hideous new judgment's coming next?

As payback for more passions I let molder,
more arts and talents I allowed to slip,
could I be doomed to gourmet-cooking shoulder,
or to the lonely anguish of flute lip?

My terrors multiply: ceramics bicep,
tap-dancing ankle, roller-skating back,
crocheting armpit, beanbag-juggling tricep
and (worst of all) mime sacroiliac.

Is there no hope for me? I toss and worry,
thoughts heavy as a monograph by Kant.
If only I could show that fateful jury
I'm more than just a flaky dilettante . . .

And then: fresh hope that justice will be carried!
I haven't stuck with hobbies, it is true—
but in the thirty years since we got married,
I've never once imagined quitting you.

Melissa Balmain

Birdwatching

When a blue jay or cardinal flits to our feeder,
no matter how raspy or shrill,
if it's lollipop-bright, a bodacious damn breeder,
it gives you a thrill.

Any goldfinch or oriole leaves you near-speechless:
"Hey—honey—oh, wow—that's so—cool!"
While I silently note that at least the thing's screechless,
you practically drool.

So it goes with each tanager, grosbeak or hummer,
but never a sparrow or wren,
as you make it quite clear that a bird is a bummer
unless it's a 10.

"See that small, subtle brown one," I say, "just like grasses
at dawn on a patch of fall ground?"
and you smile . . . but the moment a hotter one passes,
your head snaps around.

OK, fine—ogle breasts and pert tails splashed with color
in brassy and obvious form,
but remember: a mate who looks just a bit duller
still keeps the nest warm.

Reprieve

for Bill, again

Yesterday I thought you might be dying;
you couldn't do a thing I didn't love.
I rubbed your back and cooked you soup, implying
to God I had the full intention of
becoming much more saintly, there and then,
if only She would make you well again.

Today you're fine—our miracle's been granted.
I hate the way you give your soup a slurp.
Each ordinary moment feels enchanted,
although I pray you'll learn how not to burp.
I'm giddy, I'm delirious, I'm free
to be as petty as I used to be.

Melissa Balmain

Why This Is the Poem of Mine That People Will Share When I Die

It starts with trees and mulch. (Life's circle: noted!)
It doesn't dwell on government or guns,
so won't offend, no matter how you voted.
It's free of puns.

Despite its morbid title, it feels breezy,
unlikely to depress you in the least.
It isn't sexy snark you'd be uneasy
to show your priest.

This poem has no news or namechecks in it,
no clues to decade, season, week or date—
which makes it timely if I die this minute
or make you wait.

It barely mentions habits of ill breeding.
Its words are rarely of the vulgar sort.
And if you find it crap not worth rereading,
at least it's short.

Melissa Balmain is the editor-in-chief of *Light*, America's longest-running journal of comic verse. Her poems and prose have appeared in such places as *The American Bystander, McSweeney's Internet Tendency, The New Yorker, The New York Times, Poetry Daily, The Hopkins Review, Rattle,* and *The Washington Post.* Balmain is the author of two previous poetry

collections, *Walking in on People* (chosen by X.J. Kennedy for the Able Muse Book Award) and *The Witch Demands a Retraction: Fairy Tale Reboots for Adults,* as well as a travel memoir. A member of the University of Rochester's English Department since 2010, she lives nearby with her husband and (for now) one of their two children. She is a recovering mime.